The Life and Work of...

Vincent van Gogh

Sean Connolly

First published in Great Britain by
Heinemann Library,
Halley Court, Jordan Hill, Oxford OX2 8EJ
a division of Reed Educational and Professional
Publishing Ltd.
Heinemann is a registered trademark of Reed
Educational & Professional Publishing Ltd.

OXFORD   MELBOURNE   AUCKLAND
JOHANNESBURG   BLANTYRE   GABORONE
IBADAN   PORTSMOUTH (NH)   USA   CHICAGO

Designed by Celia Floyd
Illustrations by Sam Thompson
Originated by Dot Gradations
Printed in Hong Kong/China

03 02 01 00
10 9 8 7 6 5 4 3 2

ISBN 0 431 09178 1

British Library Cataloguing in Publication Data

Connolly, Sean
   Life and work of Vincent van Gogh
   1. Gogh, Vincent van, 1853-1890 – Juvenile literature
   2. Painters – Netherlands – Biography – Juvenile
   literature
   3. Painting, Modern, Dutch – Juvenile literature
   I. Title
   759.9'492

Acknowledgements
The Publishers would like to thank the following for
permission to reproduce photographs:

Page 5, Vincent van Gogh 'Self Portrait with shaven
head', Credit: The Bridgeman Art Library/Fogg Art
Museum. Page 7, Vincent van Gogh 'Milk jug',
Credit: Stichting Kröller-Müller Museum. Page 8,
Portrait Photo of van Gogh's uncle, founder of The
Hague branch of Goupil & Co., Credit: AKG. Page 9,
Vincent van Gogh 'Noon, or The Siesta, after
Millet', Credit: The Bridgeman Art Library. Page 10,
Coal mining in Belgium, Credit: AKG. Page 11,
Vincent van Gogh 'Miners' Wives', Credit: The
Bridgeman Art Library. Page 13, Vincent van Gogh
'Portrait of Theodore van Gogh', Credit: The
Bridgeman Art Library. Page 15, Vincent van Gogh
'Two Peasants Planting Potatoes', Credit: The
Bridgeman Art Library. Page 17, Vincent van Gogh
'The Allotments', Credit: The Bridgeman Art
Library. Page 19, Vincent van Gogh 'Portrait of the
Artist', Credit: Image Select. Page 21, Vincent van
Gogh 'The Night Café', Credit: B & U International.
Page 23, Vincent van Gogh 'Self-Portrait with
bandaged ear', Credit: Exley/Rosenthal. Page 25,
Vincent van Gogh 'The Asylum Garden at Arles',
Credit: The Bridgeman Art Library/Oskar Reinhart
Collection. Page 27, Vincent van Gogh 'Wheatfield
with Cypresses', Credit: AKG. Page 29, Vincent van
Gogh 'Crows over wheatfield', Credit:
Exley/Rosenthal.

Cover photograph reproduced with permission of
Bridgeman Art Library.

Our thanks to Paul Flux for his comments in the
preparation of this book.

Every effort has been made to contact copyright
holders of any material reproduced in this book.
Any omissions will be rectified in subsequent
printings if notice is given to the Publisher.

For more information about Heinemann Library
books, or to order, please telephone
+44(0)1865 888066, or send a fax to +441865 314091.
You can visit our web site at www.heinemann.co.uk

Any words appearing in the text in bold, **like this**,
are explained in the Glossary.

Contents

Who was Vincent van Gogh?

Vincent van Gogh was a Dutch artist who used paintings to show his strong feelings. He made many great paintings in his short, sad life.

4

This **self-portrait** shows Vincent aged 35, about two years before he died. He was very unhappy.

Early years

Vincent van Gogh was born in Holland on 30 March 1853. His father was a **pastor**. His younger brother Theo was one of his few friends.

Vincent was good at drawing. He made this **sketch** when he was nine years old. It shows how well he could draw what he saw around him.

Different jobs

Vincent left school when he was 15 years old. He worked in many different jobs. His uncle got him a job with an **art dealer** in London. This is a photograph of his uncle.

In his job Vincent saw paintings by many great artists. He liked a French artist called Millet. In 1890 Vincent made this painting. It looks like a painting by Millet.

Among the poor

Vincent found his work hard and lost his job. He then wanted a big change in his life. When he was 25 years old he began to **study** to be a **preacher** in a **mining** area of Belgium.

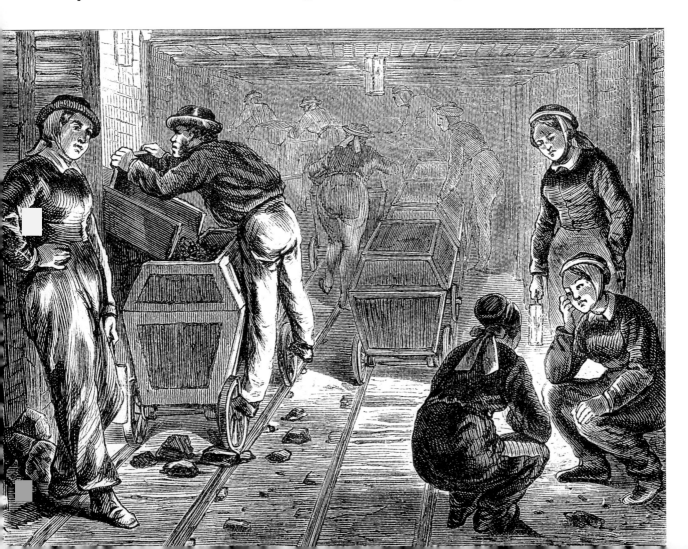

Vincent soon left these studies and went to preach to **miners**. He gave away his things to these poor people. This painting shows some of the miners' wives.

Drawing his feelings

When Vincent was 27 he gave up **preaching** and **studied** art. Then he went to join his family. Vincent's parents had moved to Etten, a small Dutch village.

Vincent argued a lot with his father and other people. Vincent shows his father's serious face in this **sketch**.

Sadness

Things got worse between Vincent and his family. Vincent left home and moved around Holland and Belgium. His father died in 1885. Vincent felt bad.

Vincent felt happier when he was able to draw and paint. He loved showing ordinary people at work.

Moving to Paris

In 1886 Vincent went to Paris to live with his brother Theo. He saw how artists called the **Impressionists** worked outside. Their paintings were full of light and colour.

Vincent also began to work outside. This is a painting of gardens in a village near Paris. Vincent used quick **brush strokes** to make the picture.

Bright colours

Theo helped Vincent meet other artists in Paris.
Vincent began to paint with bright colours. The
colours showed Vincent's moods and feelings.

18

Vincent added the bold colours of this **self-portrait** quickly and thickly. His face seems to look out through a crust of colours.

Going south

In 1888 Vincent moved to southern France. A painter called Paul Gauguin joined him in the town of Arles. Both artists loved the colourful countryside there.

Everything about the south seemed exciting to Vincent. This lively painting of a café at night shows these feelings.

Signs of trouble

Vincent often became angry or sad. Paul Gauguin left after a quarrel. Vincent felt bad almost all the time. In December 1888 he cut off part of his left ear. He was taken to hospital.

Vincent felt calm again as the ear got better.
He began to paint again. This **self-portrait**
shows the bandage on his ear.

Illness

The peace did not last long. Vincent began to hear strange voices in his head. In May 1889 he entered an **asylum** to be looked after.

Vincent felt better at the asylum. He painted there. The doctors thought this was a good idea. This painting shows the peaceful garden of the asylum.

Burst of joy

Vincent spent a year in the **asylum** and painted more than 150 pictures. He sent some to Paris but could not sell them.

Vincent's work was better than ever. The colours and curving lines of this painting seem full of his excitement.

Vincent's last days

Vincent went to live near Paris. He still painted but became sad again. Theo asked a kind doctor to help Vincent. Even the doctor could not cheer him up.

This is one of the last of Vincent's 800 paintings.
He was sad and afraid when he painted it.
Vincent shot himself on 27 July 1890 and died
two days later.

Timeline

1853   Vincent van Gogh born in Groot-Zundert, Holland on 30 March.

1865   American Civil War ends.

1869–76 Vincent works for the **art dealer** Goupil in Holland, London and Paris.

1870–71 War between France and Germany.

1876   The telephone is invented.

1877–81 Vincent trains to be a **preacher** and then lives with Belgian **miners**.

1879   The artist Paul Klee is born in Switzerland.

1881   Vincent joins his family but quarrels with his father. He travels around Holland and Belgium.

1885   Vincent's father dies.

1886   Vincent goes to live with his brother Theo in Paris.

1888   In December Vincent cuts off part of his ear.

1889   Vincent goes into an **asylum** for a year.

1890   Vincent settles in Auvers-sur-Oise near Paris in May. Vincent shoots himself and dies on 29 July.

Glossary

art dealer   person who sells paintings

asylum   hospital where people with mental illnesses get looked after

brush strokes   marks left by an artist's paint brush

Impressionists   group of artists who painted outside to make colourful pictures

miner   someone who digs for coal underground

mining   digging coal from under the ground

pastor   someone who leads a local church pictures

preacher   person who tells others about God

self-portrait   picture an artist makes of himself

sketch   another word for a drawing

study   learn about a subject

More books to read

Van Gogh, Getting to Know the World's Great Artists, Mike Venezia, Franklin Watts

Changing Colour, Looking at pictures, Joy Richardson, Franklin Watts

Tell me about Vincent van Gogh, John Malam, Evans

More paintings to see

Thatched Roofs, Vincent van Gogh, Tate Gallery, London

Farms near Auvers, Vincent van Gogh, Tate Gallery, London

The Oise at Auvers, Vincent van Gogh, Tate Gallery, London

Index